Beautiful Serenity

MAY

Emmettia A. Henderson

Scripture taken from the King James Version of the Bible.

Scripture quotations are from the ESV® Bible (The Holy Bible, English Standard Version®), copyright © 2001 by Crossway, a publishing ministry of Good News Publishers. Used by permission. All rights reserved.

Scripture quotations marked NLV are taken from the New Life Version, copyright © 1969 and 2003. Used by permission of Barbour Publishing, Inc., Uhrichsville, Ohio 44683. All rights reserved.

Scripture quotations marked (NIV) are taken from the Holy Bible, New International Version®, NIV®. Copyright © 1973, 1978, 1984, 2011 by Biblica, Inc.™ Used by permission of Zondervan. All rights reserved worldwide. www.zondervan.com The "NIV" and "New International Version" are trademarks registered in the United States Patent and Trademark Office by Biblica, Inc.™

Scripture taken from the Webster's Bible Translation.

Scripture quotations from The Authorized (King James) Version. Rights in the Authorized Version in the United Kingdom are vested in the Crown. Reproduced by permission of the Crown's patentee, Cambridge University Press.

Scripture quotations marked (CEV) are from the Contemporary English Version Copyright © 1991, 1992, 1995 by American Bible Society, Used by Permission.

Scripture quotations taken from the New American Standard Bible® (NASB), Copyright © 1960, 1962, 1963, 1968, 1971, 1972, 1973, 1975, 1977, 1995 by The Lockman Foundation Used by permission. www.Lockman.org

Scripture quotations marked (NLT) are taken from the Holy Bible, New Living Translation, copyright ©1996, 2004, 2015 by Tyndale House Foundation. Used by permission of Tyndale House Publishers, Inc., Carol Stream, Illinois 60188. All rights reserved.

WestBow Press books may be ordered through booksellers or by contacting:

WestBow Press
A Division of Thomas Nelson & Zondervan
1663 Liberty Drive
Bloomington, IN 47403
www.westbowpress.com
1 (866) 928-1240

Photograph credits: Emmettia A. Henderson

ISBN: 978-1-9736-5351-6 (sc)
ISBN: 978-1-9736-5352-3 (e)

Library of Congress Control Number: 2019901732

Print information available on the last page.

WestBow Press rev. date: 03/06/2019

WESTBOW
PRESS®
A DIVISION OF THOMAS NELSON
& ZONDERVAN

Acknowledgements

Beautiful Serenity May is dedicated to:

Mommy and Auntie

&

To all Mothers

"And these words, which I command thee this day, shall be in thine heart: And thou shalt teach them diligently unto thy children, and shalt talk of them when thou sittest in thine house, and when thou walkest by the way, and when thou liest down, and when thou risest up" Deuteronomy 6:6-7 (KJV)

_____

_____

_____

_____

_____

_____

_____

_____

_____

_____

_____

_____

_____

_____

"Honor your father and your mother, that your days may be long in the land that the Lord your God is giving you." Exodus 20:12 (ESV)

_____

_____

_____

_____

_____

_____

_____

_____

_____

_____

_____

_____

_____

_____

"She opens her mouth with wisdom, and the teaching of kindness is on her tongue."
Proverbs 31:26(ESV)

_____

_____

_____

_____

_____

_____

_____

_____

_____

_____

_____

_____

_____

_____

_____

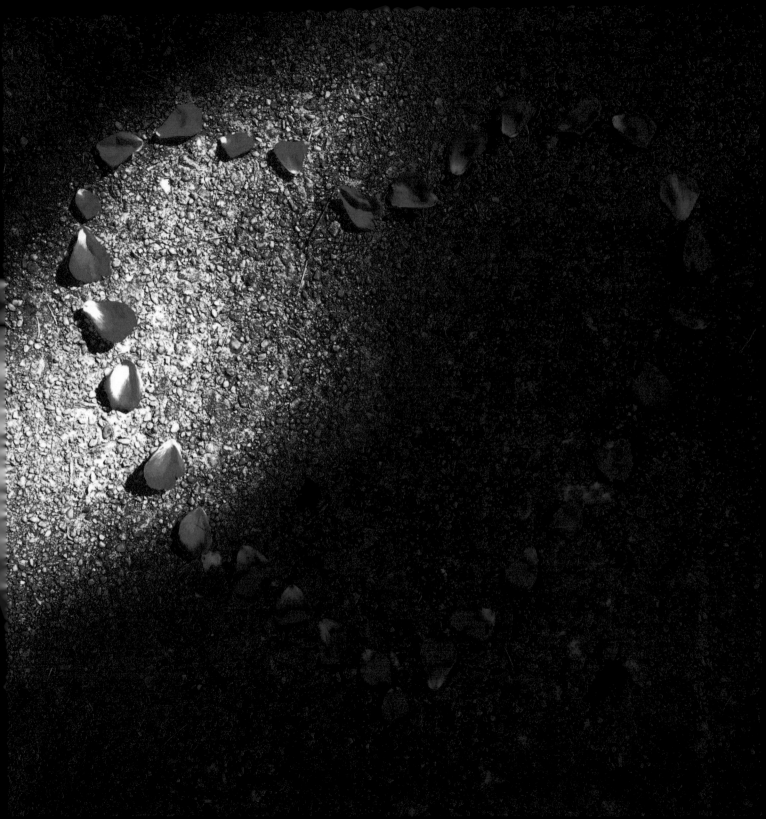

"Love is patient, love is kind. It does not envy, it does not boast, it is not proud. It does not dishonor others, it is not self-seeking, it is not easily angered, it keeps no record of wrongs. Love does not delight in evil but rejoices with the truth. It always protects, always trusts, always hopes, always perseveres." 1 Corinthians 13:4-7 (NIV)

_____

_____

_____

_____

_____

_____

_____

_____

_____

_____

_____

_____

_____

_____

_____

"Treat older women as you would your mother, and treat younger women with all purity as you would your own sisters." 1 Timothy 5:2 (NLV)

_____

_____

_____

_____

_____

_____

_____

_____

_____

_____

_____

_____

_____

_____

_____

"And Adam called his wife's name Eve, because she was the mother of all living."
Genesis 3:20 (WBT)

_____

_____

_____

_____

_____

_____

_____

_____

_____

_____

_____

_____

_____

_____

_____

"Whoever spares the rod hates their children,
but the one who loves their children is careful to discipline them."
Proverbs 13:24 (NIV)

_____

_____

_____

_____

_____

_____

_____

_____

_____

_____

_____

_____

_____

_____

"Her children arise up, and call her blessed; her husband also, and he praises her."
Proverbs 31:28 (AKJV)

_____
_____
_____
_____
_____
_____
_____
_____
_____
_____
_____
_____
_____
_____
_____

"When a wife has no children, He blesses her with some, and she is happy. Shout praises to the LORD!" Psalm 133:9 (CEV)

_____
_____
_____
_____
_____
_____
_____
_____
_____
_____
_____
_____
_____
_____
_____

"Do not forsake your mother's teaching"
Proverbs 1:8(NASB)

_____

_____

_____

_____

_____

_____

_____

_____

_____

_____

_____

_____

_____

"She is clothed with strength and dignity; she can laugh at the days to come."
Proverbs 31:25(NIV)

_____
_____
_____
_____
_____
_____
_____
_____
_____
_____
_____
_____
_____
_____
_____

"Everyone who quotes proverbs will quote this proverb about you:
"Like mother, like daughter." Ezekiel 16:44 (NIV)

_____

_____

_____

_____

_____

_____

_____

_____

_____

_____

_____

_____

_____

_____

"Rather, it should be that of your inner self, the unfading beauty of a gentle and quiet spirit, which is of great worth in God's sight."
1 Peter 3:4(NIV)

_____

_____

_____

_____

_____

_____

_____

_____

_____

_____

_____

_____

_____

_____

"Anyone who loves their father or mother more than me is not worthy of me; anyone who loves their son or daughter more than me is not worthy of me."
Matthew 10:37 (NIV)

_____
_____
_____
_____
_____
_____
_____
_____
_____
_____
_____
_____
_____
_____

"beauty is fleeting; but a woman who fears the Lord is to be praised."
Proverbs 31:30 (NIV)

_____
_____
_____
_____
_____
_____
_____
_____
_____
_____
_____
_____
_____
_____

"Direct your children onto the right path, and when they are
older, they will not leave it." Proverbs 22:6 (NLV)

_____
_____
_____
_____
_____
_____
_____
_____
_____
_____
_____
_____
_____
_____
_____

"She is more precious than jewels" Proverbs 3:15 (NIV)

_____

_____

_____

_____

_____

_____

_____

_____

_____

_____

_____

_____

_____

_____

_____

"Children are a gift of the LORD, The fruit of the womb is a reward." Psalm 127:3 (NASB)

_____

_____

_____

_____

_____

_____

_____

_____

_____

_____

_____

_____

_____

_____

"For you formed my inward parts: You knitted me together in my Mother's womb"
Psalm 139:13 (NIV)

_____
_____
_____
_____
_____
_____
_____
_____
_____
_____
_____
_____
_____
_____

"As one whom his mother comforts, so I will comfort you"
Isaiah 66:13 (NIV)

_____

_____

_____

_____

_____

_____

_____

_____

_____

_____

_____

_____

_____

_____

"Honor her for all that her hands have done,
and let her works bring her praise at the city gate."
Proverbs 31:31(NIV)

_____
_____
_____
_____
_____
_____
_____
_____
_____
_____
_____
_____
_____

"Grace to you and peace from God our Father and the Lord Jesus Christ. I thank my God every time I remember you" Philippians 1:2-3(NIV)

_____
_____
_____
_____
_____
_____
_____
_____
_____
_____
_____
_____
_____
_____
_____

"Before I was born, God chose me and called me by His marvelous grace."
Galatians 1:15(NLT)

_____

_____

_____

_____

_____

_____

_____

_____

_____

_____

_____

_____

_____

_____

_____

_____

"Can a mother forget the baby at her breast
and have no compassion on the child she has borne?
Though she may forget,
I will not forget you!"
Isaiah 49:15 (NIV)

_____

_____

_____

_____

_____

_____

_____

_____

_____

_____

_____

_____

_____

_____

"Grandchildren are the crown of the aged"
Proverbs 17:6 (NIV)

_____

_____

_____

_____

_____

_____

_____

_____

_____

_____

_____

_____

_____

_____

"Come unto me, all ye that labour and are heavy laden, and I will give you rest."
Matthew 11:28 (KJV)

_____
_____
_____
_____
_____
_____
_____
_____
_____
_____
_____
_____
_____
_____
_____

"I have loved you with an everlasting love; I have drawn you
with unfailing kindness" Jeremiah 31:3(NIV)

_____

_____

_____

_____

_____

_____

_____

_____

_____

_____

_____

_____

_____

"We love because he first loved us."
1 John 4:19(NIV)

_____
_____
_____
_____
_____
_____
_____
_____
_____
_____
_____
_____
_____
_____

"The grass withers and the flowers fall, but the word of our God endures forever."
Isaiah 40:8 (NIV)

_____

_____

_____

_____

_____

_____

_____

_____

_____

_____

_____

_____

_____

_____

"And now these three remain: faith, hope and love. But the greatest of these is love."
1 Corinthians 13:13(NIV)

_____
_____
_____
_____
_____
_____
_____
_____
_____
_____
_____
_____
_____
_____
_____
_____

"Above all, love each other deeply, because love covers over a multitude of sins."
1 Peter 4:8 (NIV)

_____

_____

_____

_____

_____

_____

_____

_____

_____

_____

_____

_____

_____

_____

"ACCEPTING THE LORD JESUS CHRIST AS MY SAVIOR"

To the Reader: Pray this prayer to the Father:

"I confess with my mouth and I believe in my heart that God raised the Lord Jesus Christ from the dead that I might be saved.

I now accept the Lord Jesus Christ as my Savior, today! Amen."

My name is _____

Today's date is _____

Printed in the United States
By Bookmasters